TOOLS FOR CAREGIVERS

- **F&P LEVEL:** A
- **WORD COUNT:** 25
- **CURRICULUM CONNECTIONS:** animals, habitats, nature

Skills to Teach

- **HIGH-FREQUENCY WORDS:** a, I, see
- **CONTENT WORDS:** cubs, lions, mane, paws, play, tail, teeth
- **PUNCTUATION:** exclamation point, periods
- **WORD STUDY:** /k/, spelled *c* (*cubs*); long /a/, spelled *ai* (*tail*); long /e/, spelled *ee* (*see, teeth*)
- **TEXT TYPE:** information report

Before Reading Activities

- Read the title and give a simple statement of the main idea.
- Have students "walk" through the book and talk about what they see in the pictures.
- Introduce new vocabulary by having students predict the first letter and locate the word in the text.
- Discuss any unfamiliar concepts that are in the text.

After Reading Activities

Explain to readers that baby lions are called cubs. Many animal babies have special names. Can readers name any other baby animals, such as puppies or kittens? Write their answers on the board. Ask readers to draw and label their favorite baby animal.

Tadpole Books are published by Jump!, 5357 Penn Avenue South, Minneapolis, MN 55419, www.jumplibrary.com

Copyright ©2024 Jump. International copyright reserved in all countries. No part of this book may be reproduced in any form without written permission from the publisher.

Editor: Jenna Gleisner **Designer:** Emma Almgren-Bersie

Photo Credits: GlobalP/iStock, cover; Eric Isselee/Shutterstock, 1, 2ml, 2br, 6–7, 10–11; Alla Tsytovich/iStock, 2tl, 12–13; Girish M P/Shutterstock, 2tr, 4–5; Wirestock/iStock, 2mr, 14–15; StuPorts/iStock, 2bl, 8–9; AndreAnita/iStock, 3; Lennjo/Shutterstock, 16.

Library of Congress Cataloging-in-Publication Data
Names: Deniston, Natalie, author.
Title: Lions / by Natalie Deniston.
Description: Minneapolis, MN: Jump!, Inc., [2024]
Series: My first animal books | Includes index.
Audience: Ages 3–6
Identifiers: LCCN 2023016719 (print)
LCCN 2023016720 (ebook)
ISBN 9798889965770 (hardcover)
ISBN 9798889965787 (paperback)
ISBN 9798889965794 (ebook)
Subjects: LCSH: Lion—Juvenile literature.
Classification: LCC QL737.C23 D464 2024 (print)
LCC QL737.C23 (ebook)
DDC 599.757—dc23/eng/20230509
LC record available at https://lccn.loc.gov/2023016719
LC ebook record available at https://lccn.loc.gov/2023016720

MY FIRST ANIMAL BOOKS

LIONS

by Natalie Deniston

TABLE OF CONTENTS

Words to Know	2
Lions	3
Let's Review!	16
Index	16

WORDS TO KNOW

cubs

mane

paws

play

tail

teeth

LIONS

I see lions.

I see a mane.

I see paws.

I see a tail.

I see cubs.

I see cubs play!

LET'S REVIEW!

Male lions have manes. Females do not. Cubs are baby lions. Look at the lions below. Which one is which?

INDEX

cubs 13, 15
mane 5
paws 7

play 15
tail 9
teeth 11